All Minds Mind

Jeena Ved

BookLeaf Publishing

India | USA | UK

Presentation by *BookLeaf Publishing*

Web: www.bookleafpub.com

E-mail: info@bookleafpub.com

ISBN: 9789363304819

First edition 2024

To all my lived experiences.

To all the poems I have read.

*To my teachers who inculcated this love of
writing.*

*And to all the poets who walked, so I can walk
too.*

ACKNOWLEDGEMENT

Thank you to my family for putting up with my eccentricities and random writing times. For not giving up on me, even when I was ready to. For reading and listening to random works at random times and still giving heartfelt feedback. A special thanks to my sister for reading, editing, the most constructive feedback, and most of all for being the biggest cheerleader of all my writings.
I wouldn't be here without you all.

PREFACE

Writing All Minds Mind has been a deeply personal journey for me. It has unfolded through years of introspection and exploration, facing highs and lows. My quest to understand myself and the intricate workings of my mind led me down various avenues—philosophy, psychology, religion, parables and spirituality. While each discipline offered some unique insights, it was the perspective of a rationalist that resonated most profoundly with me. This realisation shaped my approach to the poems in this collection, grounding them in the philosophy of the mind and self.

Throughout this process, I engaged with thought experiments and drew inspiration from the life experiences of renowned explorers, as well as my own. I slowly but surely transformed from a position of blame and conflict to that of understanding and resonance. These reflections guided me in making informed decisions about my understanding of existence and consciousness. The poems serve as an exploration of these themes. I invite the readers to join me in contemplating the complexities of thought and the nature of self.

My writing style is eclectic, reflecting a range of poetic forms—from couplets and haikus to sonnets, odes and free verse. I often found inspiration in the works of celebrated poets, sometimes choosing to echo their sentiments while at other times reinventing the wheel to express my own distinct views. This collection embodies a balance between reiterating popular opinions and presenting fresh perspectives, allowing for a dialogue between the known and the unknown.

My own experiences led me to the firm belief that while there are some core truths, nothing is really, truly absolute. I have tried to keep an open mind while exploring each theme, highlighting its strengths and vulnerabilities. I feel that on the journey to understand the human mind, it is most important to know that the mind is its own eccentric being. While there is some overlap, each mind reads in its own unique way. There are some things all of us may relate to, while others completely set us apart. Both aspects are important to accept, cherish and celebrate. When it comes to the things of the mind, no mind is all right or all wrong. We are truly beings of a grey world.

As you delve into the pages of All Minds Mind, I invite you to explore your own thoughts and feelings. Each poem is a window into the labyrinth of the human experience, encouraging you to introspect and arrive at your own conclusions. This collection is divided into eight sections, each a broad theme of an aspect of the mind and self. The sections move through starting to think, the parameters that affect thinking, the role of emotions and identity and finally diving into the more ambiguous aspects of the subconscious and transformation. This journey is not just mine – it is ours, a shared exploration of the mind and self that transcends individual narratives.

This is the first full collection of poetry that I have written and compiled. As such, it holds a special place in my heart. I hope you enjoy reading it as much as I enjoyed writing it. Please keep in mind that eventually – all minds mind. Read each poem as it speaks to you. It is not important whether you agree with me or not. It is more important that you think about each theme and form your own mind on it. Even as you know what you think today may change tomorrow, and that is ok. Together, let us navigate the chaos and beauty of existence, embracing the complexities that define our lives.

Table of Contents

a. awakening

An aware emergence awakens,
To discover an illuminated beginning,
With clarity, insights and revelations.

i.

awake

arise with gods
see the power in all
gods initiate outlook
morphing to match
changing, growing, insatiable
the old wane
from sun, moon, rain, thunder
are born their children
prosperity, longevity, destruction
the new fight for control
heavens descend
the realisation of birth
contorts to fearing death
creators and creations rage
struggling to stay awake
thinking this first spark
is the end

ah! the making
of a thinking conscious

ii.

emergence

In the stillness –
Of a void so deep,
An atom lay in silence – asleep.

A hum, a vibrating pulse,
A swirl of particles,
Shimmers and crackles.

A gathering, a colliding clash,
Molecules merge and tune,
Fervent, in life – forms maroon.

In a phenomenal phenomenon,
Cells multiply and divide,
Alive and free, seamlessly glide.

Manifestation of sentience,
From the smallest of sparks,
Played in the universe's arcs.

A testament written,
By nature's own hand,
Emergence – a wondrous psalm.

iii.

awareness

In the expanse of thought,
A pulse of understanding,
Emerging from the brought.

Each moment, a new thread,
Connections form and deepen,
As consciousness is fed.

A backdrop, vast and wide,
Each detail, a revelation,
In the currents reside.

Guiding through the haze,
Illuminating paths ahead,
In the intricate maze.

In this realm of scrolls,
Awareness, a quiet force,
Nurturing the soul.

Navigating confined,
A journey of discovery,
Where wisdom is determined.

iv.
beginning

In dawn's embrace, shadows softly fade,
A core of ice ignites in a crushing slush.
Fresh potential, a new world portrayed,
Hues of gold and rose begin the thrush.

A seedling sprouts, defying winter's chill,
Each tender shoot, a promise yet to bloom.
In whispered winds, the world begins to twill,
Awakening the heart – from silent gloom.

With every chance, life's rhythm takes flight,
As possibilities dance in morning's glow.
The past, a shadow retreating from sight,
While visions of tomorrow gently flow.

In this bright moment, hope begins to sing,
For every dawn unveils a brand new spring.

v.

discovery

In the sphere of the known,
Questions take flight,
Curiosity stirs,
Awakening insight.

A lull in quietude,
Thoughts begin to flow,
Unravelling the fabric,
Of what we seek to know.

Each layer unfolds,
Revealing hidden paths,
Connections emerge,
In the aftermath.

The thrill of the chase,
As ideas collide,
New vistas appear,
With each turn, we stride.

(contd.)

From the depths of the ocean,
To the heights of the sky,
We seek and we ponder,
With each question, we fly.

We pursue, we uncover
With fervour and might,
For in the act of discovery,
We embrace the infinite.

vi.
illumination

In the dark,
The blind grope,
Seeking and grasping,
Desperately scope.

One sees a snake,
Another, a tree trunk,
Yet another, bristles –
At a lump of hair that stunk.

One hears a snort,
Decides it is a spout,
Leaking water,
Sticky, dry and stout.

Another can feel,
A rock round,
A smooth seal,
Kneels before the mound.

(contd.)

Each convinced,
Only one to heed,
Each clings,
to this partial creed.

The whole elusive,
Hidden, beyond the reach,
The elephant sighs,
Can illumination preach?

vii.
clarity

In a fog where the lost often dwell,
Thoughts twist in a jumbled-up shell.
Like a fish in a dish,
With thoughts all a-swish,
It seeks the light – with a yell!

In a fog where confusion does creep,
Thoughts tumble and roll in a heap.
Like a fox on the hunt,
In a frantic stunt,
Finding clarity – not for the sheep!

In a mind like a jigsaw gone wild,
Thoughts scatter in a frenzy piled.
Like a clown in a gown,
With a squint and a frown,
Finding clarity – not for the mild!

In a mind like a tangled-up yarn,
Thoughts push and pull, in a barn.
Like a cat chasing light,
In a whimsical fight,
Finding clarity – a charming disarm!

viii.
insight

Einstein pondered,
Riding a beam of light,
Seeking to unravel,
Particle and wave.

The Buddha sat,
Under the Bodhi tree,
Searching for answers,
To end all misery.

Gilgamesh roamed,
Seeking immortality,
Gaining wisdom,
Of life's fragility.

Einstein's insight,
A lifetime in the making,
The Buddha's enlightenment,
Through years of aching.

(contd.)

Gilgamesh's journey,
A tale of loss and gain,
Insight's elusive,
Attained through pain.

In the dance of opposites,
Lies the path to see,
The insight of existence,
And what we're meant to be.

ix.
revelation

Howls of despair,
Illusions malign.
Forks of doubt,
This ain't right.
Open hearts,
Roaming minds,
Combine, intertwine,
Decline and Incline.

Oh! the elation
of revelation –
Eureka! Archimedes
Ran naked to define.
An apple falls,
Nature's design,
Question unasked,
Answers align.

b. existence

Imagined tangible measures,
Contemplate exhausted fragments,
In the elysium of a homeless void.

X.

measure

A second, A minute, An hour.
A year, A decade, A century.
What is the measure?
The measure of existence?

In the blink of an eye,
A lifetime may pass,
Watching the clock stand still,
As time slips through the glass.

Time's a trickster, a jester,
Toying with the sense of being,
A second an aeon,
An aeon a fleeting seeing.

The prodigal son returns,
In a heartbeat, they say,
But waits for his father,
Through an eternity's sway.

But in the end, it matters not,
If a moment's an eternity or a day.

xi.
tangible

Real?
Unreal?
Reality?
A hounding question.
A paradox unanswered.

Look up – the sky –
the roof holding up,
the very notion,
is just a reflection
of what may have been –
not too long, awhile.

Housing, the moon bright,
when it has no light, and
the stars, hard at trying,
for the tiniest shimmer,
to reach a speck of
their gargantuan worth
or their dying embers.
we'll never know,
at least not in this lifetime.

(contd.)

Look below – the ground –
trampled every day,
uncaring, like breathing –
naturally – even when without it
reality itself would have – no
leg to stand on.

Floating, that which doesn't –
yet speak the common tongue
or is beyond simple comprehension,
hinders the very concept
like it needn't be –
any part – of the greater puzzle.
All that matters – and
matters of import – no more than
a figment of allied imagination.

Like malleable clay,
and amorphous mist,
forming to fit,
and fitting to form.
Preconceived conceived conventions –
reality – an ephemeral tangibility.

xii.
imagined

In quiet corners of the mind,
Shadows dance and dreams unwind,
From whispers, hopes and fears,
Rising through the mist of years,
A tapestry of thought and lore,
An echo of what came before.

In struggles, doubts and dreams,
It mirrors back our silent screams,
A canvas painted with our plight,
A beacon in the darkest night,
In the silence, still, we find,
A figment born of humankind.

In the chaos of our days,
Shaped in a thousand ways,
A sculptor's hand, a poet's pen,
A lover's gaze, a child's grin,
In every story, every song,
Hope breathes and carries on.

(contd.)

In the depths of human thought,
In every battle bravely fought,
A spark divine in the quest for truth,
Lives the image of endless youth,
Not a being, fierce and bright,
But a reflection of its light.

xiii.

contemplation

Half the life,
Lived in silent contemplation,
Of moments lived aloud.

In quiet corners,
The mind drifts and unwinds,
Uncoiling the coiled blips.

With open eyes,
Between what is and what's in store,
A clash of wills, a tug of war.

Vivid and bright,
Collides with blinding light,
As intervals fade to grey.

In the interplay,
Of thought and deed, want and need,
Traversing between the real and the unseen.

xiv.
fragments

Cryptic fragments,
Take a toll,
Housed in the attic
– of the soul.

Gathers of dust,
Form heavy stones,
Enveloped in the silence
– of the endless epoch.

Splintered disarrays,
Make a whole,
Stitched in confusion
– of what came before.

Half-finished lines,
Shards of a voice,
Echoes of a story
– where none can remain.

xv.

exhaustion

Upright,
Stiff and steady
– Desynchronise –
A beat this way,
Ears twitch, lips in oh!
Fingers and toes follow,
Knees join, hips unsure,
Shoulders up and down,
Head completely in it,
Neck adds in a bit
– and – drop
Body falls.

In this
perfect stillness
a sparkle tinkles
in exhilarating exhaustion.

xvi.
homeless

There is –
much to express.
Much to attend.
A lot – still left unsaid.

No voice is an island.
It needs a mouth,
lips for vowels,
tongue for 'em rolls,
and a mind intent.

This voice –
unvoiced remains.
It has no home.
Mum, it chimes in vain.

xvii.
elysium

A garden of dreams,
A distant mirage,
Shadows retreat,
Sorrows find peace.

Like a hug
Of a warm gust of air,
On a chilly mountain,
With frozen feet.

Like the relief,
Of a long-held breath,
Escaping the clench,
Of a clinging stench.

Elysium whispers,
Of eternal bliss,
A promise so tempting,
Yet at what cost is this?

(contd.)

Elysium's promise,
May forever allure,
But the bliss of existence,
Is the cure to endure.

The promise of ever after,
– this life – merely a chapter.

xviii.
void

O Void,
you silent keeper,
where the echoes play,
stretched dark and deep,
existence dares to sway.

In your embrace,
the shadows linger,
a cauldron of birth,
consuming silence,
vibrating with life's pulse.

In your cradle,
the missing whispers,
the flickering dreams,
the blooming absence,
frayed with light.

In your emptiness,
a tension yearns,
a breath battles,
a flame flares,
making the fractured whole.

(contd.)

Yet, dear Void,
you are not the enemy,
nor a chasm of despair,
for your stillness confronts,
as life finds the strength to bear.

c. self

A body masks and echoes,
As desires fork and tame,
In solitude, to accept with courage.

xix.
body

Thoughts drift, realm unseen,
Flesh anchors, seeking answers,
The riddle of soul.

Philosophers ponder,
Search for the ghost of truth,
The puzzle of mysteries.

Stillness reveals light,
Body trembles, spirit soars,
The tapestry of life.

Chaos brings doubt's fire,
Can the mind heal flesh, or vice versa?
The enigma of being.

An intruder unknown,
Seeks the reason to try,
The dance of existence.

The mind and the body,
though different, are tied,
The drive of time.

XX.

fork

At every turn,
A fork presents,
Hyde playing Jekyll,
A potion brewed,
Identity splintered,
Wrong and right?

A mirror cracked,
One side murmurs,
The other shouts defiantly,
Caught in the web of choices,
The heart of Hamlet beats,
"To be or not to be?"

In fractured dreams,
A hero and a villain,
A tale with no end,
A teetotum of fate,
Heads or tails,
Which will it be?

xxi.
echoes

AAYE! Aye!, I!

In ripples of three,
Echoes linger,
And secrets creep.

"Remember when?"
Like thuds of thunder,
Seep on a gentle breeze.

The ghosts of childhood,
The weights of tomorrow,
Tease and flea.

Each bend of reflection,
Each drop of tear,
Fist and squeeze.

The armour of scars,
The corridors of choice.
Keys and crease.

Shaping the self,
That's meant to be.

xxii.

mask

Beneath the surface,
Layers unfold,
A façade crafted,
Timid and bold.

Each mask a story,
A role on display.
The jester grins wide,
Hiding the ache,
The queen stands regal,
Ready to break.

The fragments worn,
A thousand personas,
None can believe.
In time's square,
Truth and lies,
In a delicate snare.

The masks define,
The burdens bear,
Adapt and conform,
To fit the share.

xxiii.
desire

A flicker ignites,
refusing to part,
relentless and free,
a quest to be.

An ocean's pull,
a rising tide,
a compelling force,
refusing to subside.

The thrill of the ride,
with passion and pride,
a tantalising desire,
that can't be denied.

Yet, in pursuit,
an anomaly lies,
for the more it pries,
the more it defies.

xxiv.
solitude

A sanctuary
– of quiet –
the heart learns
– to breathe.

A chair
– empty –
reminding of
– all that was.

A soul
– solitary –
pauses to find
– strands of its roots.

A petal
– peels –
bending to unfold
– the strength of self.

XXV.

tame

In the quiet dawn,
A battle rages softly,
A constant, silent blur,
With currents of distraction,
It pulls away from me.

Upon the banks,
With patience as my guide,
Waves of worry crash,
Like a tempestuous tide,
"Focus!" calmness takes its hold,
– Defiant and bold.

A whirlwind of delight,
A flash of fright,
A push and pull of clarity,
Focus starts to fray,
Thoughts collide and scatter,
Like leaves blown far away.

(contd.)

Persistence wears heavy,
Stitched with threads of doubt,
Each time I try to grasp,
The cunning trickster, it slips,
In the labyrinth of thinking,
Solace and turmoil, lost in a maze.

With the resolve to try anew,
With every breath, I anchor,
To tame the wild tempest,
To steer through the clamour,
I rise every morning,
To seek the voice I hear.

xxvi.

courage

Steadfast,
breaking barriers,
keeping warm,
navigating,
craving strength,
through the doorway,
to break the mould.

An anchor,
a promise fair,
a beacon,
a reminder,
a leap of faith,
a risk to dare,
for courage
to truly care.

For some,
it comes easy,
for some,
in the bottom
of the cups.
However,
wherever,
to find it,
it's a must.

xxvii.
acceptance

In the harbour of becoming,
The ship of Theseus anchors.
Formed and conformed,
For the journey onwards,
To brace the seas and storms.

All hands on deck,
Raise the anchor,
Secure the lines,
Set the sails,
Full speed ahead.

Cast off!
The mighty Theseus drifts.
Colliding with the waves of change,
With a spirit bold and rare,
Gliding through tempests with flare.

Through surges and swells,
Planks replaced with purpose,
Sails restitched with care,
Part by part, slowly overhauled,
A legend of the past, proudly unscrawled.

(contd.)

Transformed through seasons,
Its identity redefined.
In evolving, in growing
Discovered that which resides.
Parts make a whole,
Parts fail and change,
The whole endures – ever aligned.

d. emotions

The shame of anger and grief,
Empathise with joy and pride,
Longing for the release of contentment.

xxviii.

anger

A wilful mistress,
Scared and scaring.
You seize control,
Without a knock.
Knocked out,
The self discovers,
After you recede.

A beastly protector,
Ravaging all,
In the relentless scavenge.
Impassioned fervour,
The first and final defence,
A single-strike killer,
A powerhouse,
Primed to deploy,
An absolute offering,
Of undying preservation.

(contd.)

A dear companion,
The first champion,
Keeper of sanity,
Inexhaustibly loyal,
Childishly unrestrained,
Seemingly detached.
In your blazing red path,
At your rallying command,
Free will obeys,
In your hypnotic trance.

A mature guide,
Cultivated through time,
Optimistic yet resolute,
Empathetic yet firm,
Strong yet kind,
Channelling to wield,
Locking and unlocking,
Your tireless might,
In your golden locks,
For the self to thrive.

xxix.
grief

A heavy cloak,
– settles on the soul,
Dragging down, a dark, bitter toll.

Each breath a struggle,
– each step a fight,
To navigate a path shrouded in night.

Cherished bitter tears,
– drowning in pain and fears,
The laughter shared, now a haunting refrain.

A comforting longing,
– drifting through the hollow space,
Swallowing words, making the spirit weep.

Grief is a teacher,
– harsh and unforgiving,
Stripping the layers until raw and undone.

A trust in time,
– to carry on, step by step,
The weight will ease, and the sun will shine.

XXX.
shame

A voice cruel and cold,
"You're not good enough,
– your story's been told."

Trying to hide,
To bury deep inside,
Seeping through the cracks,
– a relentless tide.

A scarlet hue,
A mark of failure,
– can't undo.

Pretending success,
Crumbling, shattered mess,
In waves, it drowns,
– of self-doubt and distress.

A prison of shame,
Worthiness can't reclaim,
– a frame of blame.

(contd.)

An innate desire flow,
A spark of courage aglow,
Trembling feet, rising head,
– a voice that says, "Let go."

xxxi.
longing

A distant echo,
A restless spirit,
Yearns to yearn,
For all that was,
And all that
– could still be.

Softly calling,
Filling the air,
A sweet ache,
A whisper of hope,
That dances just
– beyond reach.

A twitchy tide,
Pulling and pushing,
Each swell a promise,
Each retreat a sigh,
An unwavering call
– of undying aspiration.

(contd.)

A fragile thread,
Woven through time,
Binding the present,
To bridge the unknown,
Grounded in hope
– of the eternally faithful.

For in every longing,
Lies the promise
– of fulfilled becoming.

xxxii.
empathy

A listening ear,
Bridging gaps with care,
Turning silence into moments shared.

A knowing glance,
Feeling highs and lows,
Kindness in struggles, a warmth that flows.

A comforting touch,
Reaching out in need,
In compassion's membrane, hearts freed.

In everyday kindness,
A simple call to bond,
Creating connections – that go beyond.

xxxiii.
pride

Mirror's glow, shining bright,
Ambition's crown, heart on fire,
Pride dances boldly.

Victories whisper,
Lessons learned, mountains climbed,
Strength's guiding beacon.

In its prime,
Pride preservers, yet fragile,
When vanity strikes.

Ego's fortress,
Humility's shadow falls,
Connections decay.

Peacock's strutting,
Seeking praise, colours unfurled,
Essence may fade.

Quiet night's embrace,
Honour the worth, true pride's home,
Gentle, humble grace.

xxxiv.

joy

Feel it –
Its everywhere,
Seek it –
It slips away.

Catch it –
In fleeting glances,
Embrace it –
In laughter's cascade.

Hold it –
In the warmth of the sun,
Nurture it –
In the moments of play.

Share it –
With those around.
Watch it –
Brighten the grey.

(contd.)

Breathe it –
In the cool evening mist,
Trust it –
To guide your way.

Cherish it –
A balm for the spirit.
Carry it –
Timeless in its grace.

Feel it –
A radiance that stays.

XXXV.

contentment

On a cloud,
Made of marshmallow fluff,
The tea brews slowly, and the days are enough.

"Ah, contentment!",
Shout to the sky,
Pondering the meaning of "just let by."

The sun is a lemon,
The moon, a ripe pear,
The trees gossip, unaware.

The grand scheme of life,
Or the dice of a dream,
Sip my coffee, or is it whipped cream?

Contentment is simple,
As a fish that swims by,
Or a breeze that tugs at the clothes left to dry.

(contd.)

Is this bliss,
Or just a mirage?
Or rather simply escaping a barrage?

Is the cat really wise,
or just a bit stout?
Truly content, or nothing is devout?

Toast to the absurd,
To the silly and strange,
The quiet moments that need no change.

In a world that spins,
In the turbulence of delight,
Where nonsense is king, I'll be content tonight.

xxxvi.
release

Let it go,
The weight,
That you hold.

Breathe In,
The moment,
Exhale the despair.

Shake off,
The shadows,
Embrace the dawn.

Rise with,
The sun,
Where healing's begun.

Trust in,
The profound,
Its magic abound.

e. realisation

Whispers of claustrophobic validation,
An endurance of perceived cognition,
As serenity manifests with recognition.

xxxvii.
cognition

Cognition unfolds,
Thoughts take flight,
Gathering knowledge, piecing it all.

The land of perception,
Shapes reality, senses awake,
Assembling clues to colour the hues.

Here to stay,
The spotlight that guides
Grasping matter, filtering chatter.

The vault of memory,
Retrieving the past, informing the present,
A medley of learning, ever-pleasant.

The voice of language,
Ideas, symbols and sounds,
A bridge to connect, to reflect.

(contd.)

Deducing, inducing, standing tall,
From premises to conclusions,
A logical dance, to take a chance.

Imagine and decide,
Weigh the options, the pros and cons,
To blaze new trails, the wisdom to discern.

xxxviii.
whispers

In the hush of twilight,
The beginning of a sleepy night,
A voice is heard, soft as a sigh,
A whispering thought flutters by.

"Close your eyes," the whispers plead,
"Let go of the noise, the frantic speed,
In this stillness, truths will bloom,
Like flowers unfurling in a quiet room."

"Look closer," the whispers urge,
"Find the beauty in this splurge,
Where colours blend and shadows play,
The heart speaks louder than words can say."

Linger in the gentle sway,
The whispers weave their soft ballet,
In the quiet, find a spark of light,
A flickering flame in the velvet night.

(contd.)

"Create," they whisper, "let it flow,
Let the heart guide, let the spirit grow,
In this stillness, let the flames ignite,
A canvas painted bold and bright."

Breathe in deep, let the stillness unfurl,
Unhindered, the whispers begin to swirl,
In this sacred silence, I find my way,
A journey of thoughts that softly play.

But wait—what's this? A flicker of doubt,
An unreliable narrator in a familiar clout,
"Are you sure it's real—this tranquil scene?
Or just a trick of a restless machine?"

xxxix.
validation

I like This and not That
And that is ok!
I say This out loud,
And not engage with That,
– And it is still ok.

I promote This.
Hell, I even upsell,
making a whole community
of one of This gang.
This is my way,
the only way I go,
– and, yes, of course, it is ok.

I make up a tale,
passing on some rumours.
I know This is better,
even investing in an expose.
– Though a little unnecessary, it is ok.

(contd.)

Now I know for sure,
This is the best there is.
What That – could never be!
So for all to see,
Wipe its very existence, – is it ok?

For what rhyme or reason,
That should even be?
I mean, I don't like it,
and really who –
in their right mind – would!
Attack! Abolish! Amplify! Emulsify!
Why That should just let be!
– And now, it is Not ok.

xl.
claustrophobic

Descending, dark whispers.
Gong, gigantic heartbeat,
a chilling foreboding.

Running, dread grips.
Icy, claws burn,
a furling paralysis.

Beading, sweat clams.
Slick, slimy quicksand,
a bolting trepidation.

Suffocating, bind shackles.
Colossal, cosmic age,
a crippling confinement.

Shrieking, alarm shatters.
Familiar, insistent hinge,
a jolting respite.

xli.
perception

Perceived –
Perceptions belie –
Where the clock melts
And windows unravel
To kaleidoscopic views,
Under a guise
Illusions come alive,
A flicker of clarity,
Rested in absurdity,
In a delicate trace,
Irony whispers
Hiding in corners,
In a grand charade,
Spectators unwind,
Chasing the strayed,
Doubts entertain,
Shadows disguise,
Through tinted frames
Scenes unfold
And a story retold.

Perception is fickle,
– biases land in shades of grey.

xlii.

endurance

Autumn swept in the wind,
Taking the leaves away,
From lush and green –
Became the brown barren kind.
A question sprung –
Would it make roots sway?

Leaves gone and the colour lost,
Vulnerable to the surroundings,
A bare body –
Covered with frost,
A strength somewhere –
– dead inside – rose at the same.

Shivered and trembled,
Submerged in fever,
Helpless as eyes looked the other way,
Footsteps faded under the foggy cover,
In a crowded space –
Left alone, sad and grey.

(contd.)

Waiting for the spring to return,
Patiently for a call,
Prepared to –
Withstand the turn,
The turn – in time –
– For the leaves to fall.

xliii.
recognition

No hidden fears,
No borrowed light,
No shadows to chase,
No roles to play,
No labels to wear,
No past to replay.

Celebrate instead,
The beauty of now,
The essence of self,
The journey of growth,
The courage to be.

To see it clear,
To know what is real,
To welcome the truth,
To recognise me,
In the depths of my being,
In the light of my heart.

xliv.
manifestation

Minds they –

They dream bold. They
Speak gold. They

Wish wide. They
Step inside. They

Claim fate. They
Create state. They

Feel light. They
Shine bright.

xlv.
serenity

In gardens where laughter blooms,
And colours dance in joyful rooms.

With paper boats on rivers wide,
Dreams sail forth, no need to hide.

In kitchens where spices swirl and blend,
Flavours mingle, and worries mend.

With starlit skies and wishes spun,
A heartbeat whispers, "You've just begun."

f. subconscious

The surreal instinct of dreams,
String along a veiled circus,
As distractions in the labyrinth accrue.

xlvi.
strings

A stringing thought,
huddled in its own fur,
comforted by shivers,
– undisturbed – unperturbed.

Eyes watch and blink,
a wink and a squint, gazing blind.
Mouth mumbles and pouts,
a voiced yawn, gulping drool.
Skin wrinkles and scars,
a pore exposed, itching to scratch.

Nose sniffs and snorts,
an olfactory dance,
breathing in auto-mode.
Ears pitch and tone,
a rhythmic cacophony,
an eavesdropping melody.

Unmoving, statuesque,
a timed fogging of the air.
A moment still – of peace –
senseless, thoughtless, stringless.

xlvii.
circus

A tightrope sways,
Balancing dreams
Made of haze.
A magician's rabbit,
Pulled from hats,
Made of mist.

Parade of absurdities,
A flamingo dances,
A giraffe in the sky.
A monocle perched,
On a plump tabby cat,
Reciting old rhymes.

In impossible shapes,
The acrobats twist,
Both vivid and dim.
A unicycle rolls,
As thoughts crash,
Ringing in ears.

(contd.)

"The show must go on!"
The ringmaster shouts,
As the daylight is gone.
Come one, come all,
Twisted logic,
Reason confined.

xlviii.
distraction

In the ballroom,
A frenzied dance,
A whirlwind of waltz,
The next a wild tango,
The scene flits and flutters,
Unable to stay low.

Demanding attention,
Twirling and spinning,
Seeking apprehension,
As it reaches –
The height of its grace,
Another cuts in,
Stealing the space.

The music shifts,
Vying for centre stage,
A pirouette so true,
Unsure what to do,
A puppet on strings,
Pulled in all directions.

(contd.)

A daring young buck,
Leaping and bounding,
Dances with abandon,
Only to be replaced,
By a partner so grim,
A dance on the rim,
On a step-by-step tread.

Seeking to retrace,
The steps of the dance,
To find the true beat,
To find its own feet,
Grows sombre and weary,
– its focus misled.

xlix.

accrue

In the attic of the mind,
Memories gather like dust,
In corners, they sleep,
Old photographs yellowed,
Emotions like stone,
Grudges piled high,
A weight we've outgrown.

Like leaves in autumn,
They swirl, and they cling,
Each one a reminder
Of the pain that they bring,
Woven threads of regret,
In this cluttered sanctuary,
The struggle to forget.

Devotion like squirrels,
Hoarding, stashing away
The nuts of resentment
For a cold winter's day,
Burrowed deep down,
Joy fades to murmurs,
And peace finds no rest.

(contd.)

Clinging to burdens,
As if they define,
The stories to be told,
The lines entwined,
Like a garden overrun,
The beauty of growth,
Choked by needy needs.

To declutter the mind,
Is a daunting affair,
Like sorting through relics
Of love and despair.
What if we toss them?
What if we need them,
And they are no more?

Yet in the clearing,
A promise of breakthrough,
A chance to renew,
Like spring's gentle thaw
That melts winter's hold,
Releasing the past,
Letting go of the cold.

l.
labyrinth

Thoughts twist, turn,
In shadows, they yearn.
Memories drift, swirl,
In silence, they twirl.

Fears creep, crawl,
In darkness, they call.
Dreams flicker, gleam,
In fragments, they beam.

Mirrors crack, shatter,
In silence, they scatter.
Voices hum, drone,
In echoes, they moan.

Truth hides, seeks,
In chaos, it speaks.
Paths fork, divide,
In riddles, they hide.

(contd.)

Lost souls, find,
In mazes, unwind.
Whirls spin, collide,
In the labyrinth
of the subconscious
– they bide.

li.
veil

Beneath the surface,
Thoughts linger, and,
Hidden truths await.

Layers intertwine,
Colours blend in silence,
Mysteries unfold.

Glimmers of insight,
In corners of the mind,
Quietly, they shine.

Unseen currents flow,
Covertly guiding choices,
Wisdom unveiled.

A dance of the mind,
Unravelled, yet concealed,
Life's secrets revealed.

lii.
dreams

In their home,
They rest.
Feeding on
Latent secrets.

With tremors,
of hope – they rise,
Crafting new worlds,
Beneath closed eyes.

Colours entwine,
Heavy whiskers,
Echoing wishes,
That drift away.

Fleeting visions,
Dreams weave,
The heart prances,
Birthing beliefs.

liii.

instinct

In the furnace
Of the almighty
Subconscious
Bakes and Puffs
A little thing
Called Instinct.

Like a falcon,
To the falconer,
Vexed to anarchy,
When unfastened.
Fostering dread,
Fuelling amygdala.

A primal thirst,
This sixth sense,
A summons of the gut,
Untuned, unchartered,
A subcutaneous inertia,
Subtly steering –
The intuitive counsel.

liv.
surreal

In gardens of clocks,
Fish float through the air,
Time drips like honey.

Lisps of painted lips,
Kissing the sky,
Clouds bleed and blend.

A staircase spirals,
Leading to nowhere,
Climbing up the beanstalk.

In this vivid realm,
Reality bends light,
Life's canvas unfolds.

In this dreamscape,
Awake yet asleep,
The subconscious breathes.

g. unknown

The enigmatic phantom beyond,
Defeats obscure secrets,
Through uncharted, ambiguous potential.

lv.
Defeat

Whirling, swirling maelstrom.
Careening, colliding symphony.
Shards of sanity, scatter.

Frosting, plunging bedlam.
Tumbling, toppling cascade.
Confetti of calamity, consumes.

Quacking, flapping frenzy.
Soaring, ripping, upheaval.
Torrent of defiance, pleads.

Hammering, galloping, strife.
Stampeding pandemonium.
Forces of order, surrender.

lvi.
enigma

A reality exists.
Its reflection engages.
A reflection built by the mind.
A mind that builds an entire world.
A world based on individual perception.

Worlds as many,
As there are minds.
With every new birth,
So born is a new world.

In so many worlds,
Each its own reality,
How can only one supersede?
How can just one truth be?

When many can so coexist,
One as valid as the rest,
Is there really –
A room for absolutes,
Or merely – minds that overlap?

lvii.
unchartered

Vast realms lie within,
Silent currents pull and push,
Thoughts drift, undefined.

Hidden depths await,
Unseen wonders beckon,
Curiosity lures forth.

Instincts guide the way,
Through unmarked landscapes,
Unmapped quests unveiled.

In the stillness found,
Wildflowers bloom and die,
Seeking a piece of the pie.

Each turn reveals,
A seed yet to be sown,
Life's essence – unexplored.

lviii.

obscure

In corners deep where thoughts reside,
And the essence of the souls hide.

A canvas blank, untouched by light,
Where reason falters, lost from sight.

With every pulse, a question grows,
What lies beneath, no one yet knows.

The silent realms, they call to be,
Inviting thoughts to wander free.

In tangled webs of feelings might,
Unseen forces stir the night.

The heart beats loud, a steady drum,
In search of truths yet to become.

Ideas swirl like autumn leaves,
In patterns strange, the mind deceives.

(contd.)

Each flicker sparks a chance to learn,
In quiet depths, the fires burn.

In the obscure chaos, let it soar,
For in the dark, we seek for more.

lix.
phantom

Reminiscing past glories,
Yesteryears pedestaled,
Failures turn to ash,
Lessons to eyewash.

An individual's error,
Turn a life rash.
A leader in those shoes
– Tragedy for all.

A collective conscious
Turns critical –
The devil in the eyes
Sees only the devil
Far and near.

Believing in its own
Being of Godliness,
True and imagined –
The greatest vulnerability.
The reason for the downfall.

lx.

ambiguous

An eye line
How much does it see?
A bird's view,
Or does it sit closely?

The eye line –
It has a range.
A range that informs,
Inform that perceives,
Perspective that dictates,
Diktats that act,
Action the goal.

The goal –
Boils to a range,
A range – of the –
Ambiguous eye line.

lxi.
potential

Every night,
sleep comes
with the same dream –
The elves ensure,
the racks –
fill with shoes.

Yet the morning,
sees disappointing
empty shelves.
Everytime, set-up –
only to fall,
this allure of magic
that yearns to befall.

Energised –
at the notion
of a god fairy taking
away the blues.
The zeal –
deserting fast,
as reality intrudes.

(contd.)

Pull a rabbit,
Walk on clouds,
Wings to fly,
Gills to swim,
Miracles too –
have an assignment.

For now –
Potential lies
not in miracles,
As the world is awake –
awake till its retirement.

lxii.

secrets

A solid sphere
Or a coin spinning fast?

The limitation exposed.
The line stopped.
Duality merges.
Singularity splits.
A point in time
Where parallels meet.

A traveller atop a vehicle,
Partially unseen, speeding fast
Can't outrun –
The Secrets of the Path.

lxiii.
beyond

In a free fall
– a free fall,
Looking up
At a vast sky,
A sea of blue
Left behind.

Awaiting –
A hard break,
The thump
Of the destination.

Breakthrough –
The clouds that
Do not cushion.
The back refuses
To roll up and curl.

(contd.)

Hoping for spring,
Only autumn awaits.
Summer and winter
Feel the same.

As breath
Slowly abates
– this free fall.

h. transformation

Unconscious resilience evolves,
Adapts to meet revolutionary alchemy,
As metamorphosis transcends.

lxiv.
revolution

Herded around,
Pushed about,
Bell tied,
Neck ringing,
Bat beaten,
Door bolted,
– begins
A revolution.

Preachers posture,
Attitudes feature,
Hands walk,
The ill talk.
Minds bind,
Craven favour,
– the shepherd
A crusader.

lxv.
evolution

"Believe, you will be," says
The you – the I wants to be.
The I that I am
Is honestly – not so sure.

"Died, a few moments ago."
The you that wants to be
Or The I – that is?
Will that which heard – ever know?

lxvi.
resilience

Time heals all,
Tomorrow doesn't
Remember it all.

Big things pass,
The smallest try
Patience's brass.

Be the stone,
Around whom the river,
Flows in a cone.

Lying in a bed,
A bed of resilience,
Is it me
Or is it a clone?

lxvii.
adapt

Talk and rock,
And walk it off.
Redefine the past,
The Future aghast,
Lips sealed tight,
White eyes cite,
Meeting taunts,
Way beyond,
Learning to adapt –
Adapting to learn.

lxviii.
alchemy

Sounds combine –
Form letters.
Letter combine –
Become sensible.

Senses succumb –
To variety.
Lettering varies –
With geography.

The stroke –
Governs the word.
The word –
Adjusts with borders.

The meaning,
The word,
The letters,
The combines,
Modulate and mutate.
Only the sound –
– The sound –
Remains unchanged.

lxix.
meeting

I guess
   I'll meet me
When
   the time designs
And
   the stars align.

This time
   I'll begin
   With no dreams
   No silent screams
   No denials
   No passes free
   No set standards
   No being a hero
   No knight in white
   No regrets to regret

This time
   I'll try my best
   To get it right.

lxx.
metamorphosis

In the calm,
a seed takes root,
A flicker of change
– in the mind's pursuit.

Like a chrysalis
wrapped in a shell,
Ideas awaken,
– begin to dwell.

Thoughts like butterflies,
once confined and shy,
Spread their wings wide
– learning to fly.

In the furnace of struggle,
the spirit refines,
Forging new pathways,
– old beliefs decline.

Once muted and bare,
Bursts of life tread,
For in transformation,
– the mind is fed.

lxxi.

transcendence

The end is here.
It always is.
Inevitable from the start,
And just as invincible.

The makings make the man,
The man the makings.
Hoping for the other,
Fearing the one,
When only nothing –
Nothing is truly complete.

The only surety
Is the opposite,
Both sides of the coin
Are the coin itself,
And today is
Tomorrow's yesterday.
For one, it can't exist –
Without the other.

lxxii.
Unconscious

A world untamed,
A realm of whispers,
Where silence reigns,
And time disappears.

Beneath the surface,
Like ghosts in the pine,
Glimpses of the past,
Shadows of echoes cast.

Hidden desires,
A surreal ballet,
Guiding the spirits,
In a mysterious play.

A cryptic code,
Where stories unfold,
Visual sounds collide,
In this chamber, untold.

(contd.)

In the truth of our lies,
It shapes the fate,
An unseen conductor,
Weaves love and hate.

Treasure unknown,
Yearn to return,
For the magic of living
– is found in the mind.